THIS BOOK BELONGS TO

_____

Great Smoky Mountains National Park Signature Edition
Copyright © 2019 by Appleseed Press Book Publishers LLC.

This is an officially licensed book by Cider Mill Press Book Publishers LLC.

All rights reserved under the Pan-American and International Copyright Conventions.

No part of this book may be reproduced in whole or in part, scanned, photocopied, recorded, distributed in any printed or electronic form, or reproduced in any manner whatsoever, or by any information storage and retrieval system now known or hereafter invented, without express written permission of the publisher, except in the case of brief quotations embodied in critical articles and reviews.

The scanning, uploading, and distribution of this book via the Internet or via any other means without permission of the publisher is illegal and punishable by law. Please support authors' rights, and do not participate in or encourage piracy of copyrighted materials.

13-Digit ISBN: 978-1-60433-843-0
10-Digit ISBN: 1-60433-843-1

This book may be ordered by mail from the publisher. Please include $5.99 for postage and handling. Please support your local bookseller first!

Books published by Cider Mill Press Book Publishers are available at special discounts for bulk purchases in the United States by corporations, institutions, and other organizations. For more information, please contact the publisher.

Cider Mill Press Book Publishers
"Where good books are ready for press"
12 Spring Street | PO Box 454
Kennebunkport, Maine 04046
Visit us on the Web! www.cidermillpress.com

The map on the cover of this notebook was originally printed in 1953 and is included for historical reference only. Please do not use the cover image for navigational purposes when exploring Great Smoky Mountains National Park.

Typography: Georgia, Hoefler Text, and Voluta Script Pro
Image Credits: All images used under official license from Shutterstock.com
Printed in China
1 2 3 4 5 6 7 8 9 0
First Edition

GREAT SMOKY MOUNTAINS NATIONAL PARK

SIGNATURE EDITION

KENNEBUNKPORT, MAINE

Introduction

GOVERNOR PRENTICE COOPER'S SPEECH
AT THE DEDICATION OF THE GREAT SMOKY
MOUNTAINS NATIONAL PARK
SEPTEMBER 2, 1940

Mr. President, Secretary Ickes, Governor Hoey, Ladies and Gentlemen: Tennessee gladly meets with her mother-state, North Carolina, in this pleasant hour when a great national resource is dedicated by a great American—President Franklin D. Roosevelt.

If you, Mr. President, as do many others, believe with the Poet Kilmer that the tree may be lovelier than a poem, then here is a vast forest wonderland of beauty surpassing even the beauty of poetry for all Americans to enjoy.

Beneath these veil-like mists of the Great Smokies that the mountain dwelling Cherokee Indians call the Great Smoke are 129 varieties of native trees, and 18 non-native trees.

There are 200,000 acres of virgin hardwoods in this range, one of the largest stands left in America.

The lower slopes are covered by beech forests. There are fine stands of yellowwood, or "gopher trees," which, according to tradition among some of the mountain people, was the wood out of which Noah's Ark was constructed.

Some of the red spruce here are more than 400 years old.

Maple, oak, buckeye, basswood, and chestnut trees reach tremendous growth in the Great Smoky Mountains; and many shrubs of these peaks attain tree-like dimensions.

The yellow poplar or tulip tree often attains a height in this area of 200 feet, and a diameter of nine feet. More commonly found are the mountain laurel, sometimes towering to forty feet.

William Bartram, the first botanist to report in detail his findings in the Great Smoky Mountains, listed 3,710 varieties of plant life, including mosses, liverworts, fungi, lichens, and ferns; and 1,500 species of higher plant life.

In the summer months, the kaleidoscopic colors of the Great Smokies are brought out by the violets, trillium, trailing arbutus, and phlox; the azalea, wild tiger lilies, laurel, and rhododendron.

Geologists tell us that here we have the oldest mountain formation on the North American continent, and one of the oldest known to the world.

The park area is 54 miles long, 19 miles wide, contains more than 400,000 acres, and 16 of its peaks are more than 6,000 feet in height.

Within a 600 mile radius of the Great Smoky Mountains live two-thirds of the people of America.

This is among their greatest recreational assets. They are but a day and a half drive at most, or an overnight train ride, or an hour or so by plane. The park holds a major place in the entire recreational program of America.

Before establishment of the park, wildlife was being tragically depleted in this area. Now we note the satisfactory return of bears, deer, smaller furred mammals, and birds. There are 180 varieties of birds now listed in the Great Smokies, and further studies are under way. Hunting and trapping are prohibited; but during the fishing season, there are 600 miles in these mountains of what many sportsmen say are the finest trout streams in America.

Unlike the great National Parks of the West, the Great Smoky Mountains National Park is a gift of the people to the Government, not a gift of the Government to the people. The western parks were set aside from the Public Domain, whereas the lands of the Smoky Mountains Park were privately owned, and purchased with private and state funds, and deeded to the Government. Nearly $5,000,000 was raised by private donations from citizens, and from city and state appropriations. This sum was matched by the Laura Spelman Rockefeller Memorial Foundation.

This dedication today is the climax of a dream almost 50 years old.

With extreme pleasure, Tennessee joins in this ceremony of formal dedication of a great gift of the people to their fellow Americans.

The first page of the original speech given by Governor Cooper (September 2, 1940).

GOVERNOR COOPER'S SPEECH

at the dedication of the

GREAT SMOKY MOUNTAINS NATIONAL PARK

September 2, 1940

MR. PRESIDENT, SECRETARY ICKES, GOVERNOR HOEY, LADIES AND GENTLEMEN:

Tennessee gladly meets with her mother state, North Carolina, in this pleasant hour when a great national resource is dedicted by a great American -- President Franklin D. Roosevelt.

If you, Mr. President, as do many others, believe with the Poet Kilmer that a tree may be lovelier than a poem, then here is a vast forest wonderland of beauty surpassing even the beauty of poetry for all Americans to enjoy.

Beneath these veil-like mists of the Great Smokies that the mountain dwelling Cherokee Indians called the Great Smoke are 129 varieties of native trees, and 18 non-native trees.

There are 200,000 acres of virgin hardwoods in this range, one of the largest stands left in America.

The lower slopes are covered by beech forests. There are fine stands of yellowwood, or "gopher trees," which, according to tradition among some of the mountain people, was the wood out of which Noah's Ark was constructed.

Some of the red spruce here are more than 400 years old.

Maple, oak, buckeye, basswood and chestnut trees reach tremendous growth in the Great Smoky Mountains; and many shrubs of these peaks attain tree-like dimensions.

The yellow poplar or tulip tree often attains a height in this area of 200 feet, and a diameter of nine feet. More commonly found are the moun

The parks do not belong to one state or to one section...

The Yosemite, the Yellowstone, the Grand Canyon are national properties in which

every citizen has a vested interest;

they belong as much to the man of Massachusetts, of Michigan, of Florida, as they do to the people of California, of Wyoming, and of Arizona.

—Stephen T. Mather, first National Park Service Director
(1917-1929)

Anne Davis, one of the first women elected to the Tennessee State Legislation, pushed for the creation of Great Smoky Mountains National Park and helped pass a bill that purchased 78,000 acres of land from the Little River Lumber Company in 1925.

While President Calvin Coolidge signed a bill to provide for the establishment of Great Smoky Mountains National Park in 1926, the park itself was not formally established until June 15, 1934, after over 300,000 acres were purchased from local landowners.

The Great Smoky Mountains are part of the Appalachian Mountains, named for a tribe of Native Americans called the Apalachee that lived near the region. The name "Great Smoky Mountains" references the lingering fog that covers the mountains in the morning.

The Cherokee name for the mountains, "Sha-co-na-qe," means "place of blue smoke."

The park consists of 522,427 acres, including land in both North Carolina and Tennessee. The elevation of the park ranges from 857 feet at Abrams Creek to 6,643 feet at Clingmans Dome. There are over 850 miles of hiking trails throughout the park.

∞

Average Weather Conditions:

Summer Temperature
High Elevation: 51°F to 64°F
(11°C to 18°C)

Low Elevation: 59°F to 87°F
(15°C to 31°C)

Winter Temperature
High Elevation: 19°F to 35°F
(-7°C to 2°C)

Low Elevation: 28°F to 52°F
(-2°C to 11°C)

There are trees here that stood
before our forefathers ever came to this continent;
there are brooks that still run as clear as on the day the first pioneer cupped his hand and drank from them. In this Park, we shall conserve these trees, the pine, the red-bud, the dogwood, the azalea, the rhododendron, the trout, and the thrush
for the happiness of the American people.

—President Franklin D. Roosevelt, in his address at the dedication of Great Smoky Mountains National Park (September 2, 1940)

Roaring Fork is one of the larger flowing mountain streams in the park.

The Great Smoky Mountains National Park is home to over 150 cemeteries.

Clingmans Dome, the highest point in the Great Smoky Mountains, and Tennessee, is 6,643 feet tall.

The Clingmans Dome observation tower.

Great Smoky Mountains National Park has over 90 historic structures, including schools, churches, and log cabins. It has the largest collection of historic buildings on the East coast.

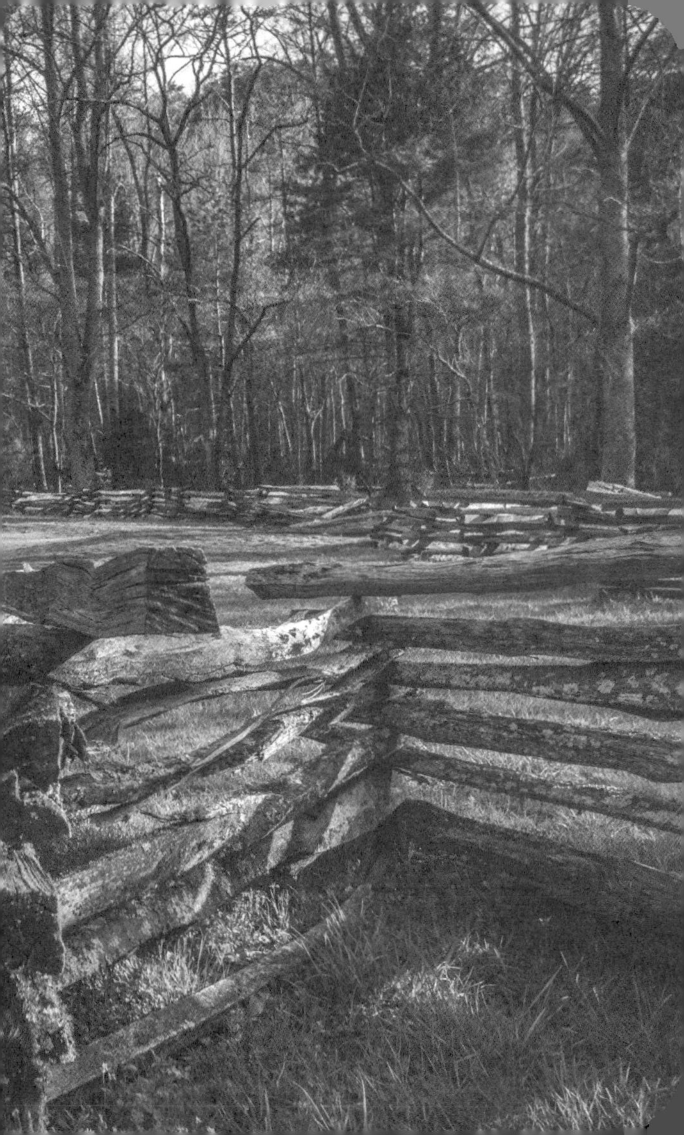

The visionaries who created Great Smoky Mountains National Park understood the power of place. They understood the way Americans draw strength from the landscapes of our continent; how

the great outdoors refuels our spirit when times are tough;

and how we cherish our connections to the mountains we hike, the rivers we fish, and the woods where we find solitude.

—Secretary of the Interior Ken Salazar, in his Great Smoky Mountains National Park Rededication speech (September 2, 2009)

I think we are all happier to know that the

solace, solitude, and beauty of wilderness

are there for whoever needs it. The next generation will need it more than we do.

—David Brower, Executive Director of the Sierra Club (1952–1969), "The Need for the National Wilderness Preservation System" (June 20-21, 1975)

Great Smoky Mountains National Park has an estimated black bear population of about 1,500, meaning there are approximately two black bears for every square mile of the park.

Climb the mountains and get their good things.

Nature's peace will flow into you as sunshine flows into trees.

The winds will blow their own freshness into you, and the storms their energy, while cares will drop away from you like the leaves of autumn.

—John Muir, *Our National Parks* (1901)

Vegetation

is to Great Smoky Mountains National Park what

granite domes and waterfalls

are to Yosemite and

geysers

are to Yellowstone.

—The National Park Service (2012)

Cades Cove is the best place to view wildlife and vegetation.

Over 1,600 species of flowering plants make their home in Great Smoky Mountains National Park.

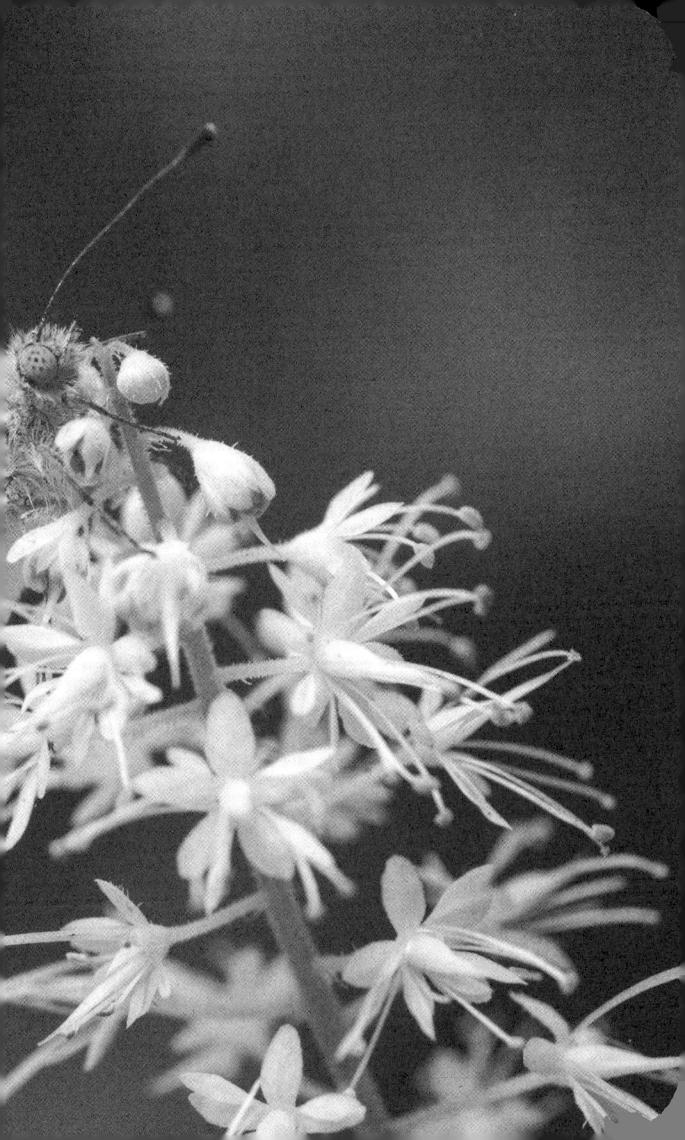

The spring brings an abundance of mountain laurel, rhododendron, and other wildflowers. In the summer months the thick forest vegetation is

lush and green.

As the leaves turn, autumnal temperatures set the mountains

ablaze in color.

—Cristine Hoyer, "A Park Ranger's Guide to the Great Smoky Mountains" (*National Geographic*, January 9, 2015)

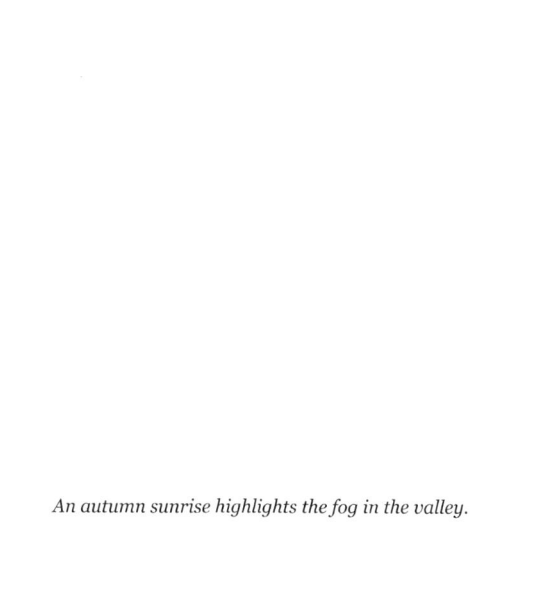

An autumn sunrise highlights the fog in the valley.

The elk is the largest mammal in the park and can weigh almost 700 pounds.

Thousands of tired, nerve-shaken, over-civilized people are beginning to find out that

going to the mountains is going home;

that wildness is a necessity; and that mountain parks and reservations are useful not only as fountains of timber and irrigating rivers, but as fountains of life.

—John Muir, *Our National Parks* (1901)

If you drive to, say, Shenandoah National Park, or the Great Smoky Mountains, you'll get some appreciation for the scale and beauty of the outdoors. When you walk into it, then you see it in a completely different way.

You discover it in a much slower, more majestic sort of way.

—Bill Bryson, *A Walk in the Woods: Rediscovering America on the Appalachian Trail* (1997)

Synchronous fireflies are the only species of firefly in America that can synchronize its flashes. They are one of 19 different species of fireflies that live in Great Smoky Mountains National Park.

∾

There are 67 unique species of fish in the park.

∾

The Great Smoky Mountains are known as the "Salamander Capital of the World," with 30 unique species making their home there.

An eastern newt.

> I just leave [the] office and go into [the] woods, get fresh balsam air, then **come back [and] start strong...**
>
> —George Masa, Great Smoky Mountains photographer, in a letter to Margaret Gooch (September, 1931)

You want a place where you can be serene…that if need be can **stir you up as you were made to be stirred up,** until you blend with the wind and water and earth you almost forgot you came from.

—David Brower, Executive Director of the Sierra Club (1952–1969), "The Need for the National Wilderness Preservation System" (June 20-21, 1975)

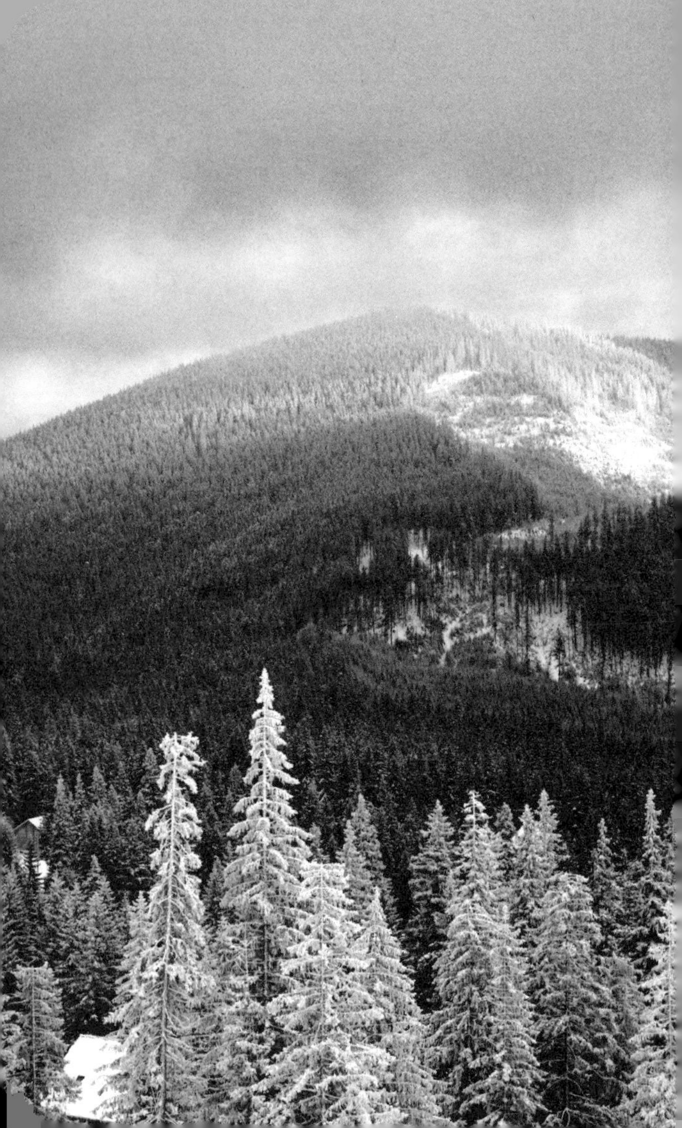

While lower regions of the park only see about 1 inch of snow during the year, Newfound Gap can get over 69 inches of snow every winter.

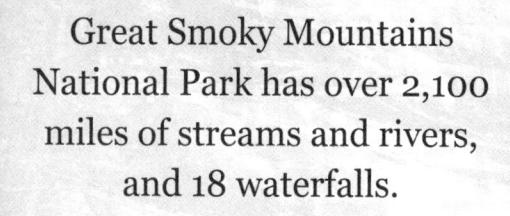

Great Smoky Mountains National Park has over 2,100 miles of streams and rivers, and 18 waterfalls.

Rainbow Falls is 80 feet high and gets its name from the rainbows that filter through the mist on sunny days.

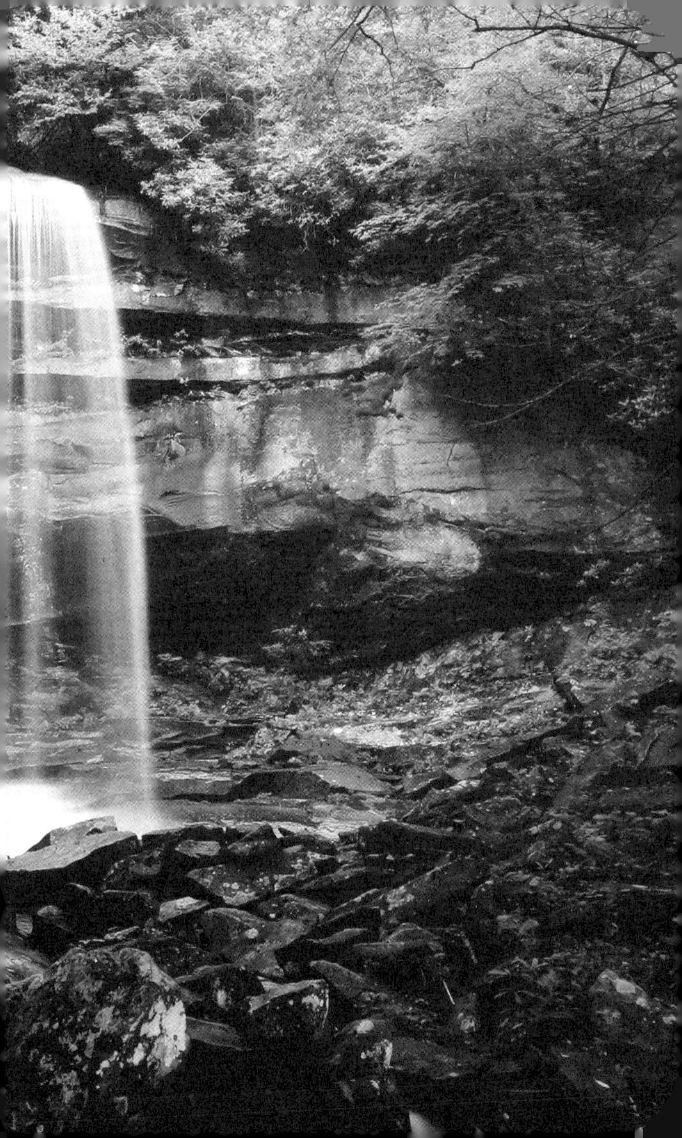

Both red and gray foxes are found in Great Smoky Mountains National Park and both prefer Cades Cove.

We get paid in sunrises and sunsets.

—A popular National Park Service employee saying

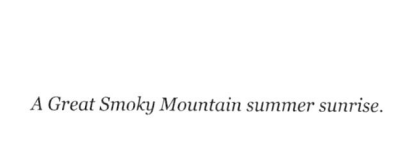

A Great Smoky Mountain summer sunrise.

The conservationist, then, is the man more concerned about what certain natural resources **do for his soul** than for his bank balance.

—David Brower, Executive Director of the Sierra Club (1952–1969), "The Need for the National Wilderness Preservation System" (June 20-21, 1975)

A pileated woodpecker.

If we have a wonderful sense of the divine, it is because we lived amid such awesome magnificence.

—Thomas Berry, *The Dream of Earth* (1988)

They will be the **outstanding scenic areas** where those from the congested centers of population...and the average fellow of the small town may....get the **recreation and inspiration** that his more fortunate brothers now get out of a visit to the Yellowstone and Yosemite.

—Arno B. Cammerer, Director of the National Park Service (1933-1940), in a letter to John D. Rockefeller (August 12, 1927)

Over 11 million people visit Great Smoky Mountains National Park each year.

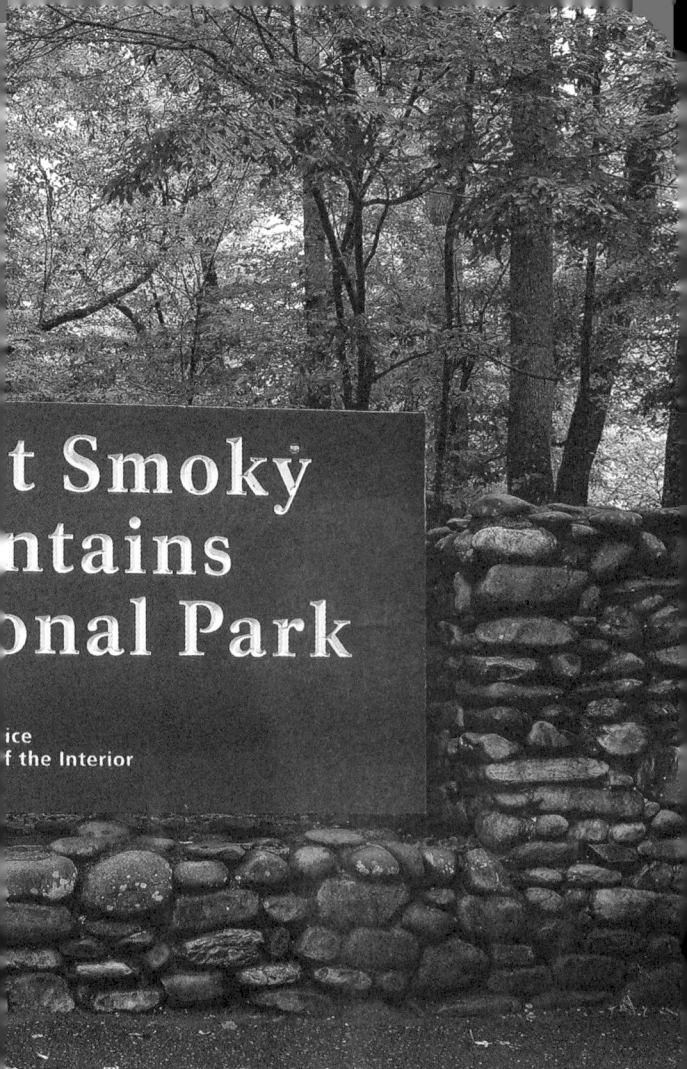

The entrance to Great Smoky Mountains National Park.

About Cider Mill Press Book Publishers

Good ideas ripen with time. From seed to harvest, Cider Mill Press brings fine reading, information, and entertainment together between the covers of its creatively crafted books. Our Cider Mill bears fruit twice a year, publishing a new crop of titles each spring and fall.

"Where Good Books Are Ready for Press"

Visit us on the Web at
www.cidermillpress.com
or write to us at
PO Box 454
12 Spring St.
Kennebunkport, Maine 04046

Millstone Gap
Tilde Ridge
Bench Mtn
Hatcher Mtn
Whiteoak Ridge
Little Rocky
Hatchertown
Stackeytown
Walland
Cove
Wasatowne
Mountain
Grapevine Ridge
Long Ridge
Rocky Mtn
Bates
Spicy Gap
W E A R
C O V E
Mt Harrison
Chinquapin Knob
Laurel Falls
Fighting Creek Gap
Metcalf Bottoms
Little River
Townsend
TUCKALEECHEE
COVE
The Sinks
Curry He Mtn
Curry She Mtn
Elkmont
Huskey Gap
Burnt Mtn
Cucumber Gap
Rich Mtn Gap
Whiteoak Sink
Cerulean Knob
Meigs Mountain
Blanket Mtn
Timber Ridge
Jakes Gap
BLOUNT CO
SEVIER CO
Tremont
Green Camp Gap
Cold Spring Knob
Ben Parton Lookout
Buckeye Gap
Cades
COVE
Anthony
Crib Gap
Cold Water Knob
Horseshoe Ridge
Thunderhead Mtn
Mount Davis
Derrick Knob
SEVIER CO
SWAIN CO
S M O
Silers Bald
TENNESSEE
NORTH CAROLINA
The Narrows
Russell Field
Mount Squires
Rocky Top
G R E A T
Blockhouse Mtn
Chestnut Ridge
Jenkins Trail Ridge
Deep Gap
Welch Ridge
Mt Glory
High Rock Ridge
High Rocks
Cold Spring Gap
Welch Bald
Bee Knob
Pilot Ridge
Round Mtn Knob
Pinnacle
Soapstone Gap
Shuckstack
Little Shuckstack
Proctor
Bearpen Gap
Matt Mtn
Welch
Walker Gap
Pullback Ridge
SWAIN CO
GRAHAM CO
FONTANA
RESERVOIR
NATIONAL
PARK
BOUNDARY
Evans Knob
Fontana Village
High Top
Perry Knob
Tommy Knob
Elk Knob
Murphy Gap
Tuskeegee